DATE DUE

Demco No. 62-0549

Reading Essentials® in Science

SCIENCE WORKS!

HEARING AND SOUND

LEWIS PARKER

PERFECTION LEARNING®

Editorial Director:	Susan C. Thies
Editor:	Lori A. Meyer
Design Director:	Randy Messer
Book Design:	Tobi Cunningham and Jason McArtor
Cover Design:	Michael A. Aspengren

A special thanks to the following for his scientific review of the book:
Kris Mandsager, Instructor of Physics and Astronomy, Mason City, IA.

Image Credits:
© Royalty-Free/CORBIS: all background images, p. 4; © Clouds Hill Imaging Ltd./CORBIS: p. 11 (top); FotoSearch.com: pp. 5, 18

Photos.com: pp. 3, 7, 9, 12, 13 (bottom), 16 (top), 17, 19, 20, 23, 24; istockphoto.com: pp. 8, 10, 21; Perfection Learning Corporation: pp. 6, 15; M. Glass: p. 16 (bottom); Liquid Library: pp. 4 (bottom), 13 (top), 14; Life ART © 2003 Lippincott, William and Wilkins: p. 11 (bottom)

For information, contact
Perfection Learning® Corporation
1000 North Second Avenue, P.O. Box 500
Logan, Iowa 51546-0500
Phone: 1-800-831-4190
Fax: 1-800-543-2745
perfectionlearning.com

1 2 3 4 5 6 PP 10 09 08 07 06 05

Paperback ISBN 0-7891-6644-5
Reinforced Library Binding ISBN 0-7569-4705-7

Table of Contents

What Is Sound ?

Sound is all around you. But what is it? What causes sound?

Sound is a type of energy caused by vibrations. Vibrations are back-and-forth movements. These vibrations cause waves.

All matter is made up of tiny particles that you cannot see called *atoms*. The atoms combine into molecules or compounds to form matter. Vibrations cause the molecules of an object to repeatedly move back and forth.

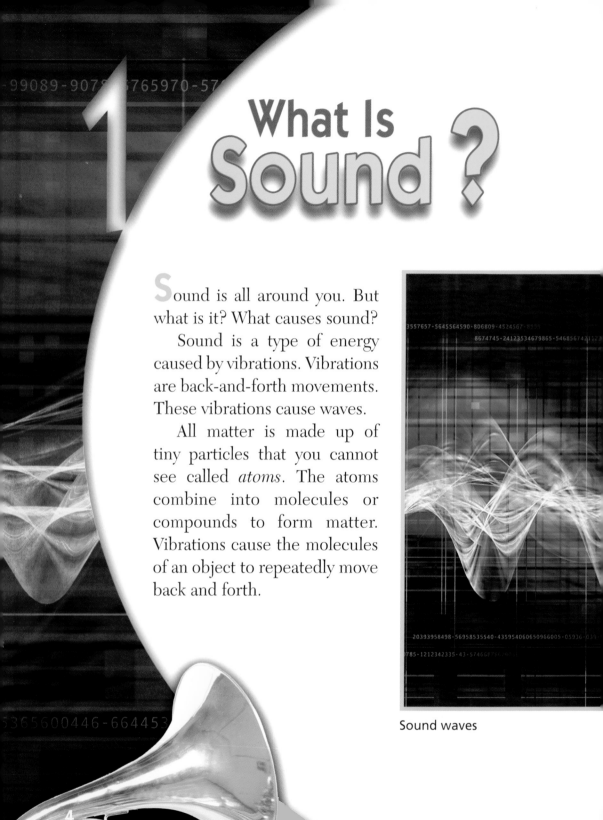

Sound waves

3557657-5645564590-806809-4524567-8959
8674745-24123534679865-5468567421123

20393958498-56958535540-435954060650966005-05936-039
0785-1212342335-43-57466786

5365600446-664453

4

Mediums

In order for these vibrations to become sound waves, they must flow through gas, liquid, or solid matter. The matter, or substance, the waves flow through is called a **medium**. The sound is carried by the medium.

Suppose you bang on a steel cooking pot. The clanging sound is made because the steel molecules in the pot vibrate, or move. The vibrations make the molecules in the air around the pot come together then move apart again. Waves are created. These moving molecules that compose sound waves carry the energy of the vibrating molecules of the steel pot right to your ears.

What was the medium for the sound of the banged cook pot? It was air. If there had been no air, there would not have been any sound when you banged on the cooking pot. Air is a gas, and most of the sounds you hear travel through air.

The speed of sound varies with each medium. Solid matter has molecules that are closer together than are the molecules in a gas or liquid, so sounds travel faster in solids.

Sounds travel slower in liquids because the molecules are farther apart. Sounds travel slowest in gases where the molecules are the farthest apart.

Inquire and Investigate: Sound Vibrations

Question: Is sound made by vibrations?

Answer the question: I think sound _is or is not_ made by vibrations.

Form a hypothesis: Sound _____ made by vibrations.

Test the hypothesis:

Materials:

- sheet of plastic
- strong rubber band
- large round cake or cookie tin
- brown sugar
- baking tray
- wooden spoon

Procedure:

1. Stretch a piece of plastic over the round tin. Place the rubber band around the outside of the tin where the plastic covers it to hold the plastic tightly in place. You have made a kind of drum with the plastic sheet as the drumhead.

2. Sprinkle a teaspoonful of brown sugar on top of the plastic.

3. Take the baking tray and hold it close to the drum. Tap the baking tray hard with the wooden spoon.

Observation: The sugar jumps up and down on top of the drumhead.

Conclusions: Sound is made by vibrations. When you hit the baking tray, the metal vibrates. It continues to vibrate for a split second after you stop. As the tray vibrates, the air around the tray also vibrates. The vibrations of the air are really sound waves. They quickly flow out in circles in all directions. You can't see these vibrations. When the sound waves hit the drumhead, they make the drumhead vibrate. The vibrations cause the sugar to jump up and down on top of the drumhead. The sugar jumping up and down are vibrations you can see. The sound waves that move out to your ear allow you to hear the tapping on the tray.

Sound Thinkers

Over the years many thinkers and scientists have added to our knowledge of sound. More than 2500 years ago, Pythagoras, a Greek, discovered something important about sound. He watched strings of different lengths vibrate. He saw that the shorter strings made higher sounds.

Two hundred years later, Aristotle, another Greek, said that sound traveled because something caused movement in the air.

About 1600, the Italian scientist Galileo experimented with sound. He used a stretched string in his experiments. He discovered that the **pitch**, how high or low the **frequency** of a sound is, depended on the length and weight of the string, and how tightly it was stretched.

A Scientist of Significance: Robert Boyle (1627–1691)

Robert Boyle, an English scientist, is credited with making one of the most important discoveries about sound. About 1660, he placed a bell in a jar and then pumped the air out of the jar. He had created a **vacuum**. Boyle set the bell to ringing. He could see the clapper on the bell clanging, but there was no sound from the bell. Boyle discovered that sound needs a gas, solid, or liquid to travel through. Without air in the jar, there was no sound.

An ambulance makes a higher-pitched sound as it approaches and a lower-pitched sound after it passes because of the Doppler effect.

In 1640, Marin Mersenne, a French scientist, figured out the speed of sound in air. He measured how long it took **echoes** to return.

The Doppler Effect

In the 1800s, Christian Doppler, a Dutch scientist, discovered an interesting behavior of sound. Doppler had two groups of musicians help him in an experiment. One group stood beside a railroad track and played their trumpets. The other group rode on a train and played their trumpets. The train roared down the track. As the train moved toward them, the musicians beside the track heard that the pitch of the moving trumpets was higher than the pitch from their own horns. Then after the train went past them, the pitch of the moving trumpets was lower than the pitch of the standing musicians' horns. But both groups had been playing the same note! This change in pitch as sound moves toward or away from the listener is called the *Doppler effect*.

How Do You Hear?

You can feel the vibrations of sounds. If you place your hand on a radio, you might be able to feel the sound vibrate in your fingertips. Or when you talk, place your fingers against your throat. You will feel your vocal cords vibrate. However, the sense of touch is not what we think of with sound. We use the sense of hearing with sound.

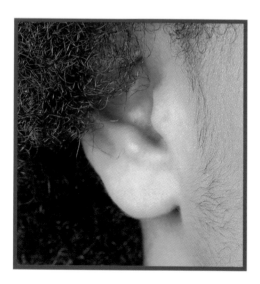

The Funnel

Your ears are a fantastic part of your body. They pick up the sounds around you and then change the sounds into a form that your brain can use. The outer part of your ear is shaped like a **funnel** to catch sound waves. Since the funnel shape of your ears faces forward, you hear sounds in front of you better than sounds behind you.

The Beat of the Eardrum

Sound waves travel into your ear canal. At the inner end of the ear canal is your eardrum. It is thin and stretched tightly like the top of a drum.

The sound waves make the eardrum vibrate. Those vibrations are passed on to the middle ear.

The Hammer, Anvil, and Stirrup

There are three tiny bones in the middle ear—the hammer, the anvil, and the stirrup. They are the three smallest bones in your body. The hammer is connected to the center of the eardrum on the inner side. When the eardrum vibrates, it moves the hammer from side to side. The other end of the hammer is attached to the anvil. The anvil is attached to the stirrup. The other end of the stirrup rests against the cochlea. So sound waves move the eardrum, which in turn moves the hammer, anvil, and stirrup. The stirrup moves back and forth, carrying the vibration to the cochlea.

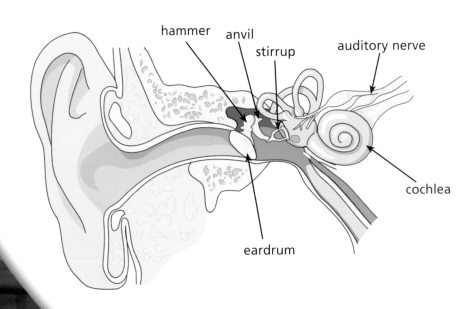

hammer   anvil   stirrup   auditory nerve   cochlea   eardrum

From the Cochlea to the Brain

The cochlea is shaped like a snail shell and is the size of a pea. It has clear liquid and tiny hair cells inside it. The stirrup causes the liquid in the cochlea to vibrate. When the liquid vibrates, the tiny hair cells move and create electrical signals.

The electrical signals travel through the auditory nerves to your brain. Your brain is like a computer. It gives meaning to the electrical signals so you hear the sound.

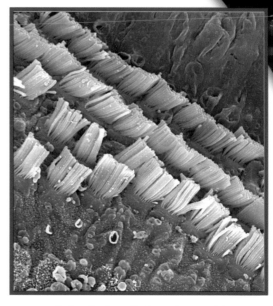

Rows of tiny hair cells line the cochlea.

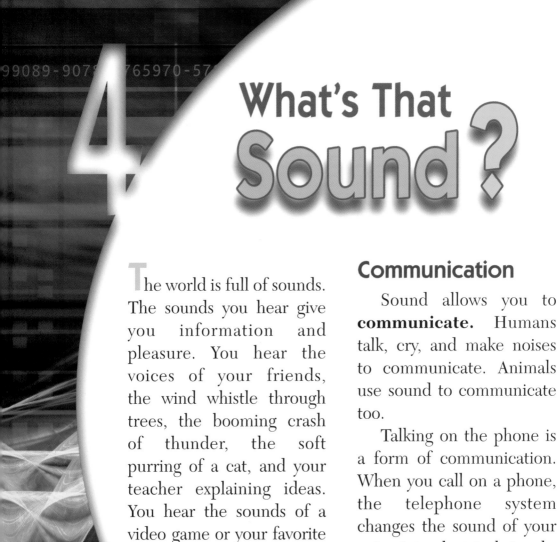

What's That Sound?

The world is full of sounds. The sounds you hear give you information and pleasure. You hear the voices of your friends, the wind whistle through trees, the booming crash of thunder, the soft purring of a cat, and your teacher explaining ideas. You hear the sounds of a video game or your favorite music on a CD.

Communication

Sound allows you to **communicate.** Humans talk, cry, and make noises to communicate. Animals use sound to communicate too.

Talking on the phone is a form of communication. When you call on a phone, the telephone system changes the sound of your voice into electrical signals. The signals flash through cables to satellites in space, so you can call anywhere in the world.

Natural Sounds

Some sounds occur naturally. They are produced by nature. The weather, natural events, or animals can cause these sounds. High winds during a hurricane may make a growling sound. A waterfall slowly trickling down a cliff can produce a pleasant, calming sound. Natural sounds also include the cracking sound of an icicle breaking or the snapping of burning logs in a fireplace. The snarl of a dog is a sound warning you to stay away from the animal. Wolves howl at the moon to communicate with other wolves.

The rush of water over waterfalls is a natural sound.

Human-Made Sounds

Humans make many sounds. Humans whistle, hum, sing, and make music that is sweet to listen to. They can also make many unpleasant sounds, such as snoring.

Humans cause other noises. The roar of a car engine, the pounding of a hammer, the crack of a bat hitting a ball, and the blare of a siren from a fire truck are all human-made sounds.

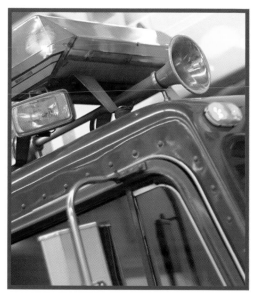

The blare of a fire engine siren is a loud human-made sound.

5 Volume, Pitch, and Frequency

Volume is a term used to describe how loud or how soft a sound is. However, the measurement of loudness is called *sound intensity level* and is measured in decibels (dB).

Any sound that is above 85 dB (decibels) can damage your hearing if you hear it long enough. With a background noise of 85 dB, you have to shout to be heard by another person. If you listen to sound that is 90 dB or more for eight hours, your ears will hurt and your hearing will be damaged. That's why you should turn down the sound on your CD player. You cannot listen to a jackhammer for very long without wearing ear

Studies have shown that people exposed to sounds over 90 dB for two hours suffer hearing loss.

Sounds with their decibel (dB) levels	
Normal breathing	10 dB
A whisper	30 dB
Normal conversation	50–65 dB
Car	70 dB
Alarm clock	80 dB
A lawn mower	85–90 dB
Jackhammer	110 dB
Live rock music	110–140 dB
Jet engine	130–140 dB

protection, or you will harm your hearing.

Pitch

Pitch is the highness or lowness of sound. The sound of a bass drum is said to have a low pitch, while the sound of a bird call is said to have a high pitch.

Some sounds have a pitch so high or so low that they are beyond your ability to hear. Certain animals can make and hear some sounds that humans can't.

Frequency

What causes a sound to be either high-pitched or low-pitched? Remember that sound is vibrations that travel in waves. The top points of the waves are called *peaks*. The peaks can be close together or farther apart. Each peak, or wave crest, represents a vibration.

The frequency of a wave is how many vibrations it makes in one second. It is measured by counting the number of wave crests, or peaks, in one second. Frequency is generally measured in what are called **hertz** (Hz).

The pitch has to do with the frequency of the sound waves. The higher the frequency of the wave, the higher the pitch we hear. So sound waves with peaks close together have a high frequency and a high pitch. The lower the frequency, the lower the pitch. That means that waves with peaks farther apart have a low frequency and a low pitch.

Have you ever noticed the strings on a guitar? Some strings are thinner than others. If you pluck a thin string, the string moves faster so it vibrates more frequently, making a high-pitched sound. If a thicker string is plucked, it moves slower so it vibrates less frequently and makes a lower-pitched sound.

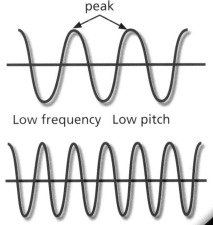

peak

Low frequency   Low pitch

High frequency   High pitch

15

Wavelength is the distance between neighboring crests, or peaks. For sound waves moving the same speed, sounds with short wavelengths are high-pitched. Sounds with long wavelengths are low-pitched. Humans hear sounds with frequencies as low as 20 Hz and as high as 20,000 Hz.

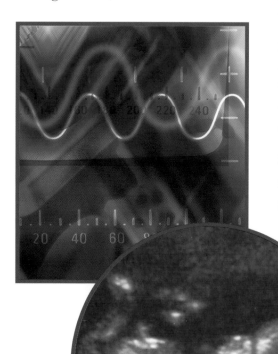

Ultrasound

There are sounds with frequencies higher than 20,000 Hz. But humans cannot hear these sounds. Sound that high is called **ultrasound**.

Animals such as dogs, bats, and dolphins can hear ultrasound. A bat cannot see very well so it finds its food by using ultrasound. As a bat flies through the night, it sends out high-pitched squeaks. These sounds bounce off the bat's supper, such as moths. The bat hears the echoes and finds its food. Ultrasound does not spread out as much as other sound. Humans have found uses for ultrasound. Builders who put up skyscrapers use echoes from ultrasound to find any cracks in the tall buildings. Doctors can send ultrasound through a person's body. Pictures from the ultrasound echoes show up on a screen so that doctors can study a person's heart, bones, and muscles.

Acoustics 6

Acoustics is the science of understanding sound. It is also the word used to describe the way sound bounces around inside a building, auditorium, or room. The acoustics differ from place to place. Buildings with a lot of echoes have poor acoustics. If the building has a lot of bare surfaces, then the echoes never seem to stop. Other places such as auditoriums are built so the acoustics are great. The audience can hear what is being said on the stage without the interference of echoes.

The Sydney Opera House in Australia

8535540-4359540606509966005-05936
842335-43-5746687867908

Echoes

Echoes are the reflections that sounds make. Echoes occur when sound waves move forward and crash into something solid. That solid could be a mountain or it could be a wall in your home. Then sound waves reflect from, or bounce off, the solid object.

Sound waves are reflected easily from solid, hard surfaces. That's why when you sing in the bathtub, your voice sounds especially powerful. The sound of your voice bounces off the tile walls.

Of course, sound is not always reflected. Sound that meets a soft surface is absorbed, or taken in. It does not bounce back to the listener. If you sing into a cushion, the sound will not bounce back. The cushion will muffle the sound. That's the reason you don't hear a lot of echoes at home. There are many soft surfaces such as rugs, sofas, curtains, and chairs to absorb sound.

Controlling Echoes

People who build concert halls and auditoriums have to design them with acoustics in mind. The echoes have to be controlled. They cannot get rid of all the echoes because that would make the sound flat and lifeless. They have to know how to use echoes to give members of the audience the best sound. Sometimes a concert hall or auditorium will have a suspended ceiling, special padding, soft seats, and boxes placed in ways to reflect sound from the stage to the audience.

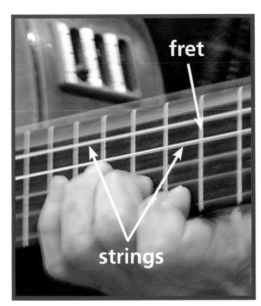

Millions of different chords can be made on a 6-string guitar.

Music! Music Everywhere!

Music is sound with frequencies that are pleasant to hear. The vibrations occur at a regular pace. Noise is just the opposite. The vibrations of noise are not at a regular pace. The sound of a cement truck is not nearly as pleasant as the sound of a flute.

Musical instruments work by pushing air around and making it vibrate. Players of musical instruments control the frequency and volume of the vibrations.

Stringed instruments, such as guitars and violins, use tight strings that vibrate to produce sounds. When the strings are stretched tighter, a high-pitched sound is produced. Changing the length of the strings can make sounds with different pitches. Pressing down the strings at certain places along the **fret** changes the length of the guitar string. This helps produce the large number of notes a guitar can make.

In wind instruments, such as a flute or oboe, the player blowing air across a hole or reed causes vibrations. In a trumpet, the player's lips pressed against the mouthpiece cause the vibrations. The vibrations create the music.

Players of percussion instruments create music by vibrating the stretched drum skin with their hands or a stick. A tighter skin on a drum gives a high-pitched note. If the skin is loose, the sound is lower.

A drumhead vibrates to create music.

Sound and Hearing

Sound makes it possible for humans and animals to communicate. Without sound, the world would be a quiet, lonely place.

Technology Link: The Synthesizer

A **synthesizer** is an invention that makes sounds electronically. Robert Moog developed the Moog synthesizer in the 1950s. His invention could only play one note at a time. Today computers control synthesizers. A synthesizer, which is one machine, can make all the sounds of a large orchestra. Many rock musicians use synthesizers in concerts instead of other instruments.

Internet Connections and Related Reading
for
Hearing and Sound

http://www.glenbrook.k12.il.us/gbssci/phys/Class/sound/u11l2a.html
This site gives information on pitch and frequency.

http://www.fi.edu/fellows/fellow2/apr99/soundindex.html
A Franklin Institute site all about sound.

http://websrv01.kidshealth.org/kid/body/ear_noSW.html
Learn all about the ear, its parts, and how it works.

http://www.smm.org/sound/nocss/top.html
Presents activities, discussions, and multimedia explorations about sound.

* * * * * * * * *

Experiments with Sound by Salvatore Tocci. Explains what sound is, how sounds are made and heard, and includes eight experiments to help understand sounds. Children's Press, 2001. ISBN 0516273531 (PB) 0516222511 (HB) [RL 4.2 IL 3–5] (6871101 PB 6871106 HB)

Hearing Things by Allan Fowler. Explores the wonders of hearing. Children's Press, 1991. ISBN 0516049097 [RL 2.3 IL K–3] (4755206 HB)

Sound by Darlene Lauw and Lim Cheng Puay. Presents activities that demonstrate how sound, especially musical sound, works in our everyday lives. Crabtree Publishing, 2002. ISBN 0778706087 [RL 4 IL 2–5] (3396401 PB)

Sound by Jason Cooper. Gives a lot of information on sound. Rourke Publishing, 1991. ISBN 0865931674 [RL 3 IL K–6] (0223606 HB)

- RL = Reading Level
- IL = Interest Level

Perfection Learning's catalog numbers are included for your ordering convenience. PB indicates paperback. HB indicates hardback.

Glossary

acoustics (uh KOO stiks) science dealing with sound

communicate (kuh MYOU nuh kayt) give or exchange information by speech or writing

echo (EH koh) reflection (bouncing back) of sound back to its source

frequency (FREE kwen see) measure of how many vibrations a wave makes in one second

fret (fret) one of a series of ridges fixed across the fingerboard of a stringed musical instrument

funnel (FUHN uhl) cone-shaped object with a large opening at the top and a small opening at the bottom

hertz (herts) unit of frequency equal to one cycle per second

medium (MEE dee uhm) substance that sound moves through

pitch (pich) measure of how high or low a sound is

synthesizer (SIN thuh seye zuhr) electronic device capable of electronically generating and modifying sounds

ultrasound (UHL truh sownd) sounds above the human hearing range

vacuum (VAK yuhm) space completely empty of matter

volume (VAHL youm) measure of how loud or soft a sound is

wavelength (WAYV length) distance between neighboring crests, or peaks, in a sound wave

Index